Bad Hair

Kay Nichols
High Point, North Carolina

Illustrations by
Catherine Ward

Dominie Press, Inc.

The development of the *Teacher's Choice Series* was supported by the Reading Recovery project at California State University, San Bernardino. All authors' royalties from the sale of the *Teacher's Choice Series* will be used to support various Reading Recovery projects.

Publisher: Raymond Yuen
Series Editor: Stanley L. Swartz
Editorial Assistant: Bob Rowland
Illustrator: Catherine Ward
Cover Designer: Steve Morris
Page Designer: Michael Khoury

Copyright © 1997 Dominie Press, Inc. All rights reserved. No part of this publication may be reproduced or transmitted in any form or by any means without permission in writing from the publisher. Reproduction of any part of this book, through photocopy, recording, or any electronic or mechanical retrieval system, without the written permission of the publisher is an infringement of the copyright law.

Published by:

Dominie Press, Inc.

1949 Kellogg Avenue
Carlsbad, California 92008 USA

ISBN 1-56270-827-9
Printed in Singapore by PH Productions Pte Ltd.
3 4 5 6 IP 03

Jan looked in the mirror. "Oh, no! It's a bad hair day," said Jan.

On the bus, she dropped her books and money. "Oh, no! It's a bad hair day," said Jan.

At her desk, she broke her blue crayon.
"Oh, no! It's a bad hair day," said Jan.

At lunch, she spilled her milk on the floor. "Oh, no! It's a bad hair day," said Jan.

On the playground, she fell over a big rock. "Oh, no! It's a bad hair day," said Jan.

When Jan got home, her Mom said, "How was your day?"

"It was a bad hair day," said Jan.

Mom said, "I had a bad hair day, too."

About the Author

Kay Nichols is a graduate of Barton College in Wilson, North Carolina. She received her Reading Recovery™ certification from the University of North Carolina, Chapel Hill, through the Randolph County training site. Kay currently teaches Reading Recovery™ and Title I Reading at Trinity Elementary School. She has taught kindergarten and the second, fourth, and fifth grades during her 24-year teaching career. Originally from Wilson, North Carolina, Kay has made her home in High Point, North Carolina with her husband, Hoyt, and her three children, Wendy, Keith, and Karen. When time permits, she enjoys reading, traveling, and going to the theater.